THE LITTLE BOOK OF HONEY

Elizabeth Gowing

design and illustrations by
Su Jones
and
Paddy McEntaggart

ELBOW PUBLISHING

This book wouldn't have been possible without Rob,
fellow-adventurer in new dishes and acquired tastes.

Thank you, too, to those who tested recipes for us and
gave us 'yummy noises' and other feedback from England,
Singapore, the USA, Australia and Kosovo:
Catherine Day, Christie Peucker, Flaurie Storie,
Leslie Postin, Marion Jones, Naomi and Maia Giaretta,
and Sharon Trudgian.

ELBOW PUBLISHING
Published by Elbow Publishing
Copyright © Elbow Publishing

ISBN 978-0-9574090-0-2

Printed and bound in Great Britain by
Ex Why Zed
www.exwhyzed.co.uk

CONTENTS

TASTING NOTES

RECIPES

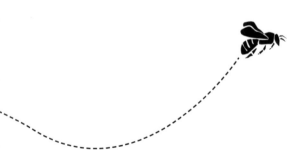

TASTING
NOTES

MY OWN HONEY

This book will take us around the world –
New Zealand to Nigeria, California to Cornwall,
with Greece, Russia, Sardinia and other bee
pastures in between – and since a good
honey has a terroir just like a good wine
we should be able to taste the earth,
the summers and the rains of all these
as we sample.

I love travelling but of course every
journey starts at home.
So let's take as our
first tasting sample
the honey I produce
in my adopted home
– the beehives on a
hillside half an hour
outside Pristina, in the
Republic of Kosovo.
The bees pasture on
wild flowers and as
I contemplate the
spoon in front of
me, I imagine those
extravagant bouquets
concentrated onto one
little spoon.

I've been taught to judge my honey first by its colour. Mine is light amber.

Then aroma? I'm getting caramel, and something ever so slightly medicinal (I'm guessing there was thyme growing near the hives).

Flavour. Oh good, I get to taste it now. The first sensation of course isn't taste, but the bulk of the cool spoonful, the feel of it dissolving at blood temperature, flooding your mouth. This honey has floral tones, something almost as sweet as rosewater, and a lingering fruity taste, like a very ripe nectarine. Lovely.

Finally, absence of defects? That's where I fall down. When we harvested this honey, we forgot to put the muslin in the sieve. The little golden tongue of the honey licked out from the centrifuge spout and down through the wide-mesh sieve and into the jar while we were still fussing around about our equipment. I reckoned it didn't matter if there was a speck of propolis here or there (it is supposed to have wonderful curative properties) and that it would be easy to fish things out later, but the flotsam has remained in the jar, held like a fly in (light) amber.

SUNFLOWER HONEY

If you could taste sunshine, what would it taste like?
Yellow things - lemon and butter and pineapple -
and green things: cut grass, new figs. That's what
sunflower honey tastes of.

It's the colour of sunshine too - a thick yolky honey
that's sweet as summer, bright as the shades on a
child's drawing. I'm tempted to daub my fingers with
it and smudge a cartoon smily face at the top
right hand corner of a page.

This is honey that's wasted on you
during the summer. You should
cap the jar shut quickly, and store
up that rich yellow stuff like a
small bright solar cell in your
cupboard, laid up against
the winter days when there
will be nothing
streaming

through the window
except a thin mean
draught. That's the
magic of honey
- that it can
bloom when
the flowers that
produced it have
wilted, a taste
blossoming on
the tongue and the
plate when the tall
nodding plants who
gave up their nectar
for it have wizened, sagged
and been
cut down.

Then you can open up the cupboard and hold out
your crock of sunflower honey gold like proof to
yourself in midwinter. Summer was here, and this is
how summer can come again.

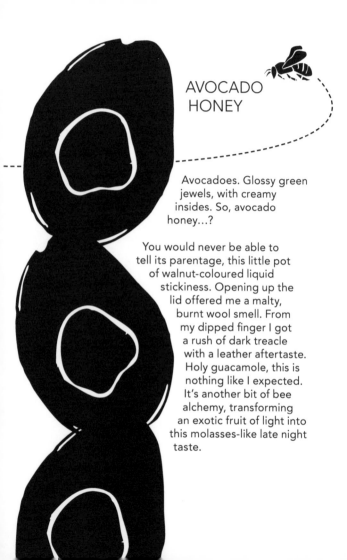

AVOCADO HONEY

Avocadoes. Glossy green jewels, with creamy insides. So, avocado honey…?

You would never be able to tell its parentage, this little pot of walnut-coloured liquid stickiness. Opening up the lid offered me a malty, burnt wool smell. From my dipped finger I got a rush of dark treacle with a leather aftertaste. Holy guacamole, this is nothing like I expected. It's another bit of bee alchemy, transforming an exotic fruit of light into this molasses-like late night taste.

So what to do with it? This is no chirpy breakfast honey, or afternoon tea drizzle; this needs a dish built around it, or to contribute to a sophisticated dessert. I'm a vegetarian, so I left off glazing sausages years ago, but if I were still to be honey-glazing meat I think this would work very well. Likewise it would go with the witchy pleasures of stewed prunes (I'll cut it with some crème fraîche or yoghurt), with anything containing cloves, with chestnuts or trickled over chocolate ice-cream.

BEECHWOOD HONEY; THE SPOONFUL OF SUGAR AND THE MEDICINE THAT GOES DOWN

What would you rather: 100 cups of green tea or one pot of honey?

Actually, that sounds like the way a James Bond villain with a strange taste in health foods might offer to kill you – a choice between the bitter gagging of too many cups of green tea or the sweet nausea of a whole pot of honey – but my New Zealand Beechwood honey says on the label that one 500g pot has as many antioxidants as 100 cups of green tea. And the honey is an awful lot tastier than the tea, though there is still something nagging like a nanny over its sweetness, that tells you it must be good for you.

The smell is warm, buttery and vaguely medicinal; can you imagine heating up some fudge in a pan that had previously been used for a TCP gargle? Then you dip your finger into the very fluid (some beechwood honeys never crystallise) amber liquid, exactly the colour of Dettol. So it's no surprise that the taste carries the same slight tang, though we have moved along the scale from phenol to mellowed whiskey.

Given that description, I can't quite see why I find this honey so extraordinarily more-ish. After all, if I wanted buttery without the medicinal oddness, I could gorge on clover honey (see p. 32); if I wanted mellowed whiskey tones with no phenol I could dip again and again into my pot of vintage honey (see p. 26) – perhaps it's a Puritan streak in me that makes me relish the fact that it should be good for me. Certainly, more than almost any other honey I've tried, this one is what I keep going back to for just one more lick of the spoon. Something I have never ever done when I'm drinking green tea.

CORIANDER HONEY

If I said that the scent of this honey reminds me of furniture polish, then I hope you'll take it more as a compliment to my (beeswax-based) furniture polish than as a criticism of the foodstuff. The aroma is spicy and complicated. Knowing what the label says, I could believe I can scent coriander in there - the musk of the seeds and the paraffin kick of the leaves. I could believe there were lots of things in there, but you would never suspect it was honey.

So when I put some in my mouth the sweetness is a surprise; furniture polish never tasted like this. But the relative simplicity of the flavour is also a disappointment after those complex and competing wafts from the jar.

Only on the aftertaste – what lingers around the tastebuds at the back of your mouth as you swallow - do you start to get more interesting flavours. The lanolin that is usually present only in the scent of a honey now asserts itself, with a smoky finish.

I think this honey should be used for something special. Maybe it would go with tofu and ginger, maintaining the Asian theme of the flowers from which it was harvested.

Or maybe it would bring up the sheen on the mahogany gate-legged table in our sitting room?

TRUFFLE LAVENDER HONEY

From Philadelphia someone brought me back this little pot of wonder.

I admit that when I saw the label I sneered a little. Truffle lavender honey seems, well, over-complicated. I know from Norfolk that lavender honey is wonderful. Truffles are wonderful. But putting them together? It's like the people who produce strange cheese from a perfectly good white Stilton with stupid blueberries squashed into it. It's over-engineering the combination of some rather exclusive flavours. It's…

I was still muttering such things as I opened the pot. And then I stopped.

Truffle gives me a solar plexus kick like only one other flavour I know (coriander). And the impact of truffle is not just in the taste, but also in the smell. I'm used to the smelling of food being a polite, maybe academic activity. It's the postponement of pleasure, the 'opening act you have to sit through before Pink Floyd comes on.' But truffle-sniffing. That could be a full-time hobby on its own for me. I breathed deeply.

And then I stuck my finger in the pot and got the full benefits of the mixture of smoky lavender and earthy truffle, with a melody of ripe fruit sweetness from the honey. I gather that in the Garce's Trading Company restaurant, where this honey was bought, they serve it with Manchego cheese, and I can see that would work well. But who needs the cheese? I just kept dipping my finger in the honey, again and again.

REGENT'S PARK HONEY

What do you know about Regent's Park? For me it is Open Air Shakespeare, and Elizabeth Barrett Browning walking her dog. It's the zoo and herbaceous borders; it's a huge gothic drinking fountain and a rose garden to hear secrets in. Now, what would all of those things taste like?

I'm learning to take a bee's approach to life. 'Yes, you may be very beautiful, you blowsy hybrid bloom, but what's your nectar like?' Not just me - as city gardeners become more aware of the flowers that offer the nectar that bees need, city honey is becoming more and more prized. Where country 'wildflower' honey may in fact offer nectars from a limited range of hedgerow flowers that are still reeling from decades of pesticide use, honey produced by city bees can combine nectar-rich varieties such as cosmos, geraniums, mint, rhododendron, sunflower and wallflowers that can grow all together in carefully-tended gardens.

So what does Regent's Park taste like? It has a caramel scent with a herbal edge to it - smelling like a delicious mild cough pastille. The taste is different of course, with dominant citrus and raspberry leaf flavours.

It's an extremely fine honey and though I know it would taste fabulous in sandwiches, I'm trying to think of a serving that would be worthy of it (this is, after all, the honey made from the flowers in the park where Elizabeth Barrett Browning walked her dog). It would go well in baking, with nuts (I'm itching to try it with almonds, for example) and its lemony tones would team brilliantly with ginger. But I am being tempted to some crazier combinations. Drizzled on broccoli, for example? Maybe with the ginger too?

THE HONEY THAT'S BETTER THAN CHOCOLATE. REALLY

So can you guess where this honey comes from…?

It's a yolky yellow colour. That's no help.

And the smell: Malt, and burnt caramel.

In the mouth, there is a slightly granular consistency, a mellow sweetness, and a coffee aftertaste.

That aftertaste, together with the smell is the clue – this is honey from nectar collected from carob flowers.

I remember carob from 1980s health food shops where I was assured that it was a substitute for chocolate. The people who say that are like people who say margarine is a substitute for butter. The word we use for people like them is 'liars'; I've never been a big fan of carob, but carob honey is something else. I don't say this lightly, but I think carob honey might be better than chocolate. I'll just scoop another fingerful to check that I'm right…

FAIRY TALE HONEY?
VIPER'S BUGLOSS

The little box arrived through the post for me from New Zealand. Inside was a small jar labelled 'viper's bugloss' and a note to say that the jar came, as it might do in a fairy tale, from 'J Friend and Co'. It might as well have a note on it saying, 'Eat me'.

I did eat it and discovered a fairy tale taste - waxy honey almost without a scent but with a butterscotch and ripe banana taste which lasts even as it's swallowed. In case you didn't know, viper's bugloss is not a curse but an attractive flower, and this is a high quality honey, organic and produced by a company with CarboNZero certification.

Given that a Spanish cave painting shows honey being collected 8000 years ago, New Zealand's entry into the honey market in 1839 is a very recent development. Honey bees aren't native to New Zealand, and only when one Mary Bumby (good name for a bee-trafficker) brought a basket hive of bees over with her in the nineteenth century was there the first chance of honey like this. I thank Mary Bumby and all her fellow beekeepers and honey harvesters since – for the work which culminated in this magical pot.

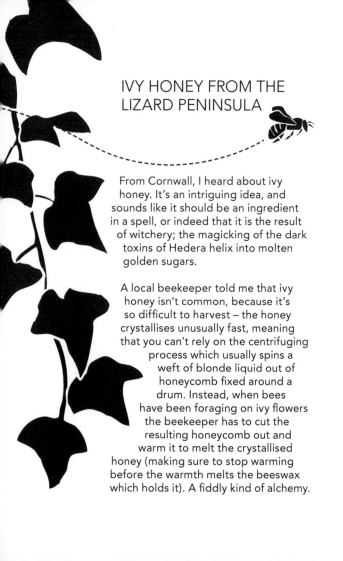

IVY HONEY FROM THE LIZARD PENINSULA

From Cornwall, I heard about ivy honey. It's an intriguing idea, and sounds like it should be an ingredient in a spell, or indeed that it is the result of witchery; the magicking of the dark toxins of Hedera helix into molten golden sugars.

A local beekeeper told me that ivy honey isn't common, because it's so difficult to harvest – the honey crystallises unusually fast, meaning that you can't rely on the centrifuging process which usually spins a weft of blonde liquid out of honeycomb fixed around a drum. Instead, when bees have been foraging on ivy flowers the beekeeper has to cut the resulting honeycomb out and warm it to melt the crystallised honey (making sure to stop warming before the warmth melts the beeswax which holds it). A fiddly kind of alchemy.

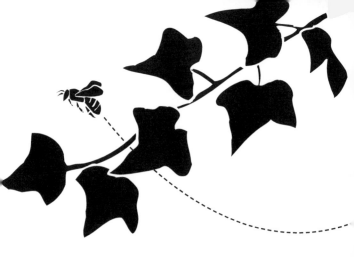

And is it worth it? I approached the pot of ivy honey I ordered online from the Lizard Peninsula (which is exactly the kind of address a honey witch would give) with some trepidation. It's a dark, toffee-coloured honey, waxy in consistency. The aroma is surprisingly flowery and light, but the taste is certainly not. It's not a very sweet honey, and there is a bitter kick in it which hits you as the crystallised paste melts in your mouth.

I tried to place the flavour and then I got it – if a pointy-chinned woman got out her wand and turned a Stilton into a honey, this is what it would taste like.

And is that a good thing? I'm not convinced.

OUT OF DATE?
VINTAGE LONDON HONEY

The story goes that when Tutankhamun's tomb was being excavated, some intriguing ancient jars were discovered. On opening them up, the archaeologists found they were full of something dark and sticky and liquid, sweet-smelling. Having poked a nervous finger into the jar an archaeologist lifted the liquid to his lips and announced that it was honey, and delicious. The jar was brought back to the lab for further analysis and on closer inspection it was found that, deep inside, in a slow – very slow – marinade within the honey, were the well-preserved vital organs of some four thousand year old member of the court.

Are you feeling queasy?

But it all goes to show that honey is an excellent preservative. And that when the Cotswold Bees company markets 'vintage London honey' it doesn't mean they are selling off out of date stock. However, looking at the jar you could imagine that Anubis might have presided over its sealing. The contents are dark and mysterious.

The aroma is malty and musky – late autumn leaves in scent as well as colour. It's a pleasingly fluid honey though – not the encrusted crystals you might imagine if you'd dug out a twenty-one year old jar from the back of your cupboard.

Twenty-one years! It is some kind of miracle that this honey is here. I try to remember what the summer of 1991 was like. Bryan Adams, the Gulf War, John McCarthy's release, and Time's Arrow. What did it taste like?

It's not as sweet as my memories. This honey is tinged with nostalgia in its mellowed caramel tobacco flavours, though its aftertaste is as strong and sweet as the first tones on your tastebuds. But of course what we're getting now is in fact the aftertaste – the flavour that has lingered for a score of years, over half my lifetime. This honey is as delicious a concept as it is a richly flavoured treat.

DANDELION HONEY

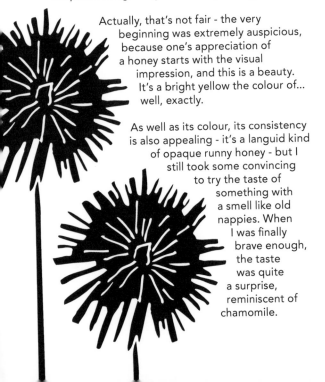

Dandelions are also known as piss-a-beds. I have no idea what the chemical or folklore connection might be, but when I lifted the lid on my pot of dandelion honey I got a powerful whiff of ammonia. It's not an auspicious beginning for a honey tasting.

Actually, that's not fair - the very beginning was extremely auspicious, because one's appreciation of a honey starts with the visual impression, and this is a beauty. It's a bright yellow the colour of... well, exactly.

As well as its colour, its consistency is also appealing - it's a languid kind of opaque runny honey - but I still took some convincing to try the taste of something with a smell like old nappies. When I was finally brave enough, the taste was quite a surprise, reminiscent of chamomile.

The honey isn't particularly sweet, and it's cool on the palate, leaving a strange almost oily residue. This is less a honey than an experience.

I can't honestly believe I will ever reach for this pot to spread it on toast, lick it off a spoon or drizzle it over anything, but I can imagine that the taste will combine well to make something like a salad dressing (see p. 72), where very sweet honeys can be egregious. And it would be no bad thing for that aroma to be mixed with some vinegar before it's brought to table.

BEES ABROAD –
THE NIGERIAN HONEY

I've never been to Nigeria so opening this pot of
honey is the first direct contact for my senses with
a country half a world away. And I had been right
to expect a taste that seemed to come from
far away; an exotic spicy muskiness.

What the scent of this honey most
reminds me of is sandalwood,
and that fragrant wood shares
its colour with this honey. The
same family of aromas linger
in the taste too – the first
taste is of tamarinds and
then there's something
like cardamom with a
leathery finish. I'd like
to use the honey as a
marinade or caramelize
onions in it and eat with
a fresh cheese.

I'm glad that this
honey tastes special,
because it represents

a very special group of projects, using beekeeping to fight poverty in Africa and beyond. I was sent the honey by one of the project leaders of Bees Abroad. Through her I learned about work in Kilimanjaro where the charity supports spinally injured women to become beekeepers, and their women's beekeeper groups in Zambia. The start-up capital needed for a beekeeper in these countries is small - £30 will buy the materials to build a hive, as well as providing a smoker and the materials needed for marketing – and as any beekeeper knows, the rewards can be great. Not just financial rewards for the individual, but the psychological rewards of feeling part of the workings of a small and harmonious community, the environmental rewards of supporting a healthy ecosystem – and then the tongue-tingling rewards of eating that fabulous honey.

CLOVER HONEY;
MY MOTHER'S TRUE STORY

I vividly remember sitting in front of a pot of clover honey as a child and asking my mother why it had a picture of a flower on it (this was in the same kitchen, so I know that it was at the same age, that I was asking the uncomfortable questions about where beefburgers came from which led to me having been a vegetarian for the last 34 years).

Clover I recognised because we had it in our garden, and my mother explained that it was from those flowers that bees made this honey. It seemed a ridiculous idea (it reminds me now of the conversation I witnessed between an earnest friend and his 4-year-old son who was asking how the tide came in. Dave explained about the moon and the pull on the water, and neap and spring tides, and when he'd finished little Alfie looked at him and giggled. 'Don't be silly, Daddy!').

I remember pulling apart a clover flower shortly after this conversation with my mother, and concentrating very carefully as I nibbled the tiny ends which I had been told ('don't be silly, Mummy!') contained the sugars which the bees collected to produce that pot I'd dipped into over breakfast. Hmm. There was, yes, a vague sweetness, but the claim that from this came my spoonful of pale creamy, buttery, slightly spicy honey was quite clearly just one of those fibs that adults told you.

In fact, bees have to visit 100 000 flowers for 10 grams of honey, so if I'd thought to multiply the taste I'd had from the clover petals, and then to reduce it as thousands of tiny wings reduce it by fanning to evaporate the water, my mother's story becomes more believable.

But it's good to retain that childish sense of awe before the miracle that is honey. And good to savour, as I did 34 years ago, the cool spoonful of clover honey. It's sweet and light, with a citrus tang which changes to a sourish aftertaste that stops it being sickly to eat. Just as each of us has a deep instinctive association with the word 'mother' based on the woman who cared for us when we were first constructing our names for the world, each of us has an 'Ur' honey against which we judge all others. Clover is mine; you never forget your first honey.

BEEKEEPING FOR SOCIAL CHANGE: GOLDEN COMPANY HONEY

Zoe Palmer says you can't have attitude when you're around bees. So beekeeping is sometimes exactly the discipline needed by young people in communities like Hackney. Since 2009 Zoe's organization has engaged as 'Bee Guardians' 40 young people including young carers, referrals from the Hackney Youth Offending Team and young people who are not in education, employment, or training. Their stories and the organisation's GOLDEN values (Greatness/ Opportunity/ Learning/ Discipline/ Employment/ Nature) are inspiring. Also inspiring is the work that the Golden Company does for the inner city environment, through its twinning of City of London organizations with beehives tended by the Bee Guardians, for which urban wildflower meadows and bee friendly herbs are planted at suitable locations nearby.

And what does their honey taste like?

Just as inspiring. The pot I have was harvested from hives in St Mary's Secret Garden behind the Jeffrye Museum. It's has a lazy viscosity and a great colour: the colour of the middle traffic light, which goes with its butterscotch aroma, slightly citrus kick on first tasting, and apricot aftertastes. This honey, and the project that produced it, is a great reminder in the city to change down a gear and prepare to stop.

THISTLE HONEY

Eeyore knew what he was doing.
Feasting on thistles sounds like
a hair shirt of a treat, but – as
I should have predicted from
the sweet edge that often
emerges from the old
donkey's prickliness – thistle
honey is a delicacy.

I looked up the honey in the wonderful
Dictionary of Honey from Nomadic Bees
(Corraini Edizioni, 2008) where I learned
how bees appreciate thistles because
of their flowering at times when other
blooms are rare. And the dictionary
told me that the honey would taste of
white pepper and geraniums. Frankly, it
seemed unlikely.

I spooned some into my mouth. It was
fragrant, spicy, reminiscent of… wait
a minute – this honey really does taste
like geraniums. My mind boggles; so what would
geranium honey taste of?

ASPHODEL HONEY
FOR THOSE LIVING A LIFE
OF EQUAL GOOD AND EVIL

This honey comes from the asphodel flower of
Sardinia - a kind of narcissus, and a flower we had
better get used to: I learned today that according to
the ancient Greeks it is asphodel meadows which are
the resting place of the souls of people who've lived
lives of equal good and evil. Surely that's most people
then?

Well, I'm quite happy to spend
eternity among the flowers
which produce this distinctive
honey (or at least as happy as I
am to spend eternity in any
one place… do you think the
asphodel meadows would have
a bookshop?). It's very
rare – I had to order
mine online – and has
an exotic quality
which comes
both from its
extraordinary
crunchy texture
and its fine taste.

The scent is, if not a precise balance of good and evil, at least a bizarre metallic chamomile followed by orange blossom. The jammy taste has a creamy subtle sweet finish that the *Dizionario Dei Mieli Nomadi* describes surprisingly accurately as 'almond milk'.

I'm not going to sit on the fence (as if the asphodel meadows would have a fence) between equal good and evil: I'm a fan of this honey. If you're a beekeeper who can find an asphodel meadow while you're still alive, I'd advise you to take your hives there and look forward to the treat you have in store.

GREEK PINE TREE HONEY

They say that it's hard to leave Greece because your feet get stuck in its honey. I do love Greece, and I love that within the first few kilometers from port, airport or road border on arrival in Greece you are struck by the delicious smell; the air almost squeaks with pine resin. I take deep breaths, and when I get my chance to eat the honey made by bees foraging on these same trees, I take deep gulps of that too.

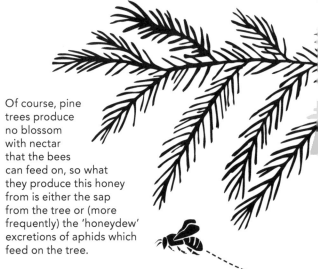

Of course, pine
trees produce
no blossom
with nectar
that the bees
can feed on, so what
they produce this honey
from is either the sap
from the tree or (more
frequently) the 'honeydew'
excretions of aphids which
feed on the tree.

Pine tree honey tastes exactly as you'd expect,
thinking of the forest - the sweetness overlaid with
a medicinal zing, and a liquorice tang that makes it
really interesting for combining with other foods.
Best of all, in my opinion, is the Greek pine tree honey
drizzled over the cool whiteness of Greek yoghurt.

I gather that in France this honey is used to make
gingerbread at Christmas and I can imagine that
would be a deeply rich and sticky treat. Added to any
dish with spices the taste would intensify. But maybe
it's just as effective to incorporate this somehow
pagan taste in a recipe that is (whether literally or not)
vanilla – for example it would transform the innocence
of a honey ice-cream (see p. 64) that's made with
a light acacia or similar honey, into a more wicked
dinner dessert.

APPLE BLOSSOM HONEY

What's the best honey to have with a croissant? It's the kind of thing you can find time to ponder on a Sunday morning.

In the end, like a little bee, I settle on apple blossom. This produces a sweet honey but the cidery scent undercuts that before it becomes cloying. And the taste has a sour apple after-kick underneath the floral sweetness. I smear it thick and translucent over butter on warm pastry.

RECIPES

CHALLAH

Challah is a Jewish braided bread eaten on the
Sabbath and on holidays. This recipe bakes it with
honey, and comes out golden and delicious. It
makes enough for two small loaves.

Ingredients:
1 tbsp yeast
1¼ cups warm water
2 eggs, beaten
⅓ cup of vegetable oil
3 tsp honey
2 tsp salt
5-7 cups flour
1 yolk, beaten

(optional)
sesame seeds

Dissolve yeast in warm water.
Add eggs, oil, honey, salt and 3 cups of flour.

Mix, and gradually add more flour until the dough is stiff.

Place remaining flour on surface and knead the dough into it until it is smooth and the flour is absorbed. If it's still sticky, add more flour.

Place dough in a large bowl covered with oiled plastic and allow to rise in a warm place for 1½ hours.

Punch down and divide into 6 portions. Twist each portion into a rope an inch in diameter and make loaves by braiding three ropes for each.

Place each loaf in a pan and allow to rise for 45 minutes. Brush top with egg yolk (and sesame seeds if you like). Bake at 190 degrees C for 15-20 minutes or until golden brown.

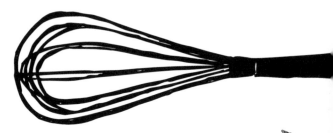

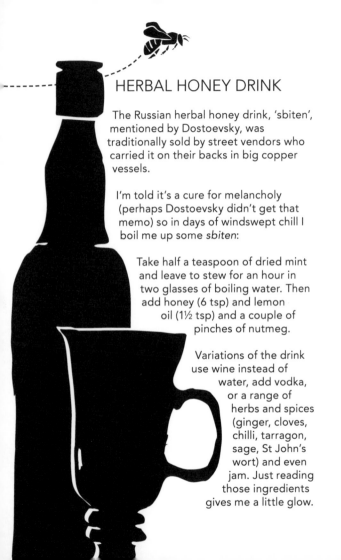

HERBAL HONEY DRINK

The Russian herbal honey drink, 'sbiten', mentioned by Dostoevsky, was traditionally sold by street vendors who carried it on their backs in big copper vessels.

I'm told it's a cure for melancholy (perhaps Dostoevsky didn't get that memo) so in days of windswept chill I boil me up some *sbiten*:

Take half a teaspoon of dried mint and leave to stew for an hour in two glasses of boiling water. Then add honey (6 tsp) and lemon oil (1½ tsp) and a couple of pinches of nutmeg.

Variations of the drink use wine instead of water, add vodka, or a range of herbs and spices (ginger, cloves, chilli, tarragon, sage, St John's wort) and even jam. Just reading those ingredients gives me a little glow.

WALNUT AND HONEY PIKELETS

What's a pikelet? A little pike of course...

And also a rich pancake/ drop scone kind of thing, which I'm told is a favourite in New Zealand and Australia.

This recipe is really easy and combines honey in the mixture, but is also wonderful served with honey (and crème fraîche). It makes approx 8-10 small pikelets.

Ingredients:
⅓ cup ground walnuts
1½ tbsp melted butter
½ cup milk
¾ cup plain flour
1 tbsp baking powder
1 tbsp honey
1 egg

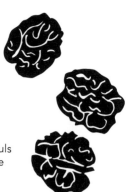

Blend all the ingredients until smooth. Cook in small spoonfuls on a lightly greased pan. Serve warm with honey and crème fraîche.

STEWED QUINCE WITH HONEY

Quinces are full of surprises. If you've ever been lucky enough to have one in your garden you'll know that during the summer you bask in their exotic blossom and feel depressed when it falls in autumn and the trees start to bud and bunion into odd knobbly almost-pears. And then just as you feel that nature in its haggard old end-of-year state can hold no joy for you, you chance to walk past the quince tree close enough for your nose to pick up from the fruit a memory of summer and more. The scent of the quince is exquisite – floral and light and almost spicy. You look at the unprepossessing fruit and sniff again. Yes! It's like catching a farmer's wife in the fields wearing Chanel No. 5.

Even the sight of them, aglow in the market in the chilly winter months lifts the heart; they could be lightbulbs taken down from a movie star's dressing room mirror; you want to buy one just to walk along the darkening street with it in your pocket like carrying a pomander or a hand-warmer.

Some people (those who aren't 'supertasters' squeamish about bitterness) can eat quince raw, though the flesh is as tough and tart as that farmer's wife.

Better to stew the quince - with honey – but prepare yourself for more surprises. You are always warned of how dangerous it is to cook quinces because of the tendency of the flesh to spatter as it's heated. It's best to wear rubber gloves and use a long spoon, as if you were to sup with the devil, though it seems ridiculous to be kitted out as if you were scared of germ warfare, while the kitchen fills with the gentle fragrance of apple and elderflower.

Peel, core and dice the quince and add about the same amount of honey as quince and enough water to cover it, just. Then heat it up together until the quince softens and the liquid reduces. It's good on its own, or mixed with crème fraîche to make a delicious fool.

YEMENI HONEY BREAD

If language were entirely onomatopoeic then I'm sure that 'yemen' would be the word for 'to eat'; saying it makes your mouth move in the same way that it does when it's savouring something really tasty. This is a recipe for Yemeni honey bread, 'bint al-sahn'.

Ingredients:
1 packet yeast
½ cup warm water
5 eggs
2 tbsp milk
5-6 cups flour
½ tsp salt
1¼ cups butter, melted
1 cup honey

Dissolve yeast in warm water then mix with eggs and milk. In a separate bowl, mix together flour and salt and form a well in the middle.
Pour the yeast mixture into the well and stir into a dough; knead dough adding ¼ cup melted butter. Knead until a smooth elastic dough results (you may need to add more flour). Cover and allow to rest in a warm place for 1 hour.

Divide the dough into 12 balls and place on a floured surface; cover with a damp towel and allow them to rest for another half hour.

Roll each ball of dough into an 8 inch circle. Place one circle into a buttered cake tin and brush with melted butter. Add 5 more circles, buttering each, and pressing the edges so the circles adhere. In a second buttered cake tin, repeat with the remaining 6 circles.

Mix the remaining butter with honey and brush the top of each stack with some of the honey-butter mixture.

Bake at 175 degrees C for 25 minutes or until the top layer is golden.

Remove from the oven and pour the remaining butter-honey mixture over both tins. Allow to cool for 20 minutes and then slice into wedges.

STEWED APPLE AND GINGER WITH HONEY

On some mornings it seems the only thing stewing may be the commuters in traffic jams, but stewing apples is more productive.

Take your pick of the apples to be stewed – fresh apples or the spongy blonde dried rings you get in British health food shops, or the dried apple you can buy in Balkan markets - leathery old curled up slices with the skin still on them, the colour of tobacco. These are attic apples, musty and sour. When I tried eating them by the handful they made my mouth pucker.

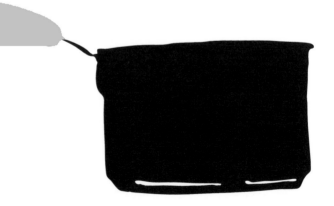

But stewed slowly, and in water sweetened with honey, they mellow. I like them with a forest honey, and give it a kick with some grated ginger. I boil and simmer the ingredients together, until the air in the kitchen is sweet and steamy, with the faint urine tang that apple and honey has.

The withered apples plump up in the water and when the fruit has reduced to something spicy and sticky I take it off the heat.

You can eat the delicious mixture on oats as a tasty breakfast and leave some left to be eaten with custard or yoghurt at lunchtime. Best of all, leave some for a bowl for breakfast the next morning, and by leaving the juices standing, the ginger steeping in the honey liquid, the apples slowly swelling further, you might find it's even better for keeping.

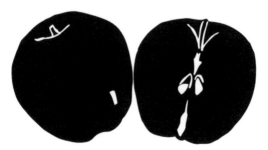

MANUKA HONEY AND BEE POLLEN IN A FRUIT SMOOTHIE

Manuka honey is the cure-all of the decade. Not only is it full of anti-oxidants, but claims have been made for it as a beater of bacteria as fearsome as MRSA, and suitable for topical application in the treatment of burns, and even in anti-ageing masks for the skin.

Mix it with fruit juice (I tried pear, orange and ginger juice) and you can't help feel virtuous. If you also sprinkle on the top some bee pollen (the bees' source of protein, gathered direct from flowers. It's stored, along with honey for energy, in their honeycomb and from here the beekeeper can harvest it just like honey) then you've treated every part of your body. The pollen adds a frothy consistency to the sweet, zingy, nutritious, just faintly medicinal drink.

Just listing the ingredients makes me feel like I've been for a run - along a beach - followed by a yoga session, and a shower; this is glowing health in a glass. I don't know what you imagine the elixir of eternal life to taste like, but surely it should bubble and zing like this drink does.

HONEY CREAM
WITH RASPBERRIES

I learned the recipe for honey
cream with raspberries from a Kosovan
recipe book (*The Kosovan Kitchen*).
'Cream and honey' is an Albanian
expression for indulgence (one step
richer than 'milk and honey')

Ingredients:
2¼ cups raspberries
1¾ cups cream cheese
1½ tbsp lemon juice
1½ tbsp vanilla sugar
6 tbsp honey

Wash and drain the raspberries. Mash half of them
with a fork and keep to one side.

Combine the other half
of the raspberries with
the other ingredients,
and spoon into tall
glasses.

Top with the mashed
raspberries.

AUSTERITY HONEY BISCUITS

Beekeeping in Britain peaked during the sugar rationing of the 1940s until there were one million hives in the UK, with their honey spread among a much smaller population than the quarter of a million hives in existence today. The reasons are obvious - when your government, like a strict nanny, is allowing you only a limited amount of sweet stuff then there's an incentive for finding alternative sources.

The Ministry of Food leaflets from the time encouraged this kind of creativity. Read today, recipes with dried egg, one-pot meals (sponge steaming in a tin in the middle of a pan while vegetables boil in the water around it), and potato biscuits have a retro chic (though I'm less convinced by advice to leave cheese in an airy place so it hardens and becomes more economical to use). The leaflets are illustrated with drawings showing women with tiny waists and frilly pinnies tied round them. And the honey biscuits are great:

Ingredients:
2½ oz (⅓ cup) margarine
1 oz (2¼ tbsp) sugar
2 tbsp honey
6 oz (1⅓ cup) self-raising flour
1 tsp cinnamon
pinch of salt.

Cream the margarine and sugar.

Add the honey and work in the flour, cinnamon and salt.

Roll out until ¼ inch thick. Cut into rounds, place on a baking sheet, and bake in a moderately hot oven for 10 minutes.

I found I needed a little more fat in order to bind the dough together (when I discovered this, I thought of my counterpart from 70 years ago, panicking having already used up more than half their weekly ration of marge) and I failed to roll out the dough as thin as ¼ inch, which meant I made only about 20 biscuits, but they tasted excellent.

BAKLAVA

This honey pastry is found all over the countries of the former Ottoman Empire including north Africa, the Middle East and the Balkans. My recipe is based on one dictated to me by my Serbian teacher, who had it from her Gorani grandmother. I buy the filo pastry though those women made their own.

Ingredients:
330g filo pastry
1 cup butter, melted
2 cups chopped nuts
⅔ cup honey

Variations make it distinctive in different countries through alterations to the nuts used (my favourite is the entirely non-traditional version with pecans, but you can also use pistachio or walnuts) and the flavourings in the syrup. I think this should be 100% honey rather than sugar, for the most intense flavour, and I like it combined with lemon or orange juice. Some people add rosewater or vanilla, and I like it with cinnamon.

The baklava is traditionally cooked in a round baking tray with steep sides. The sides are important as you will be pouring syrup into the tray to the depth of the baklava. When you have found an appropriate tray, grease it in preparation for the baklava.

Take a sheet of filo pastry and slather it with melted butter. Lay one more sheet of filo on top and again slather with melted butter. Repeat so you have a stack, three sheets thick.

Spread the crushed nuts of your choice along one third of the length of the filo stack. Roll the pastry as tight as possible around the crushed nuts and continue rolling until you have a long cylinder. Cut this into pieces which are as long as your baking tray is high (perhaps 4cm) and take the small cylinders you've produced and snuggle them into the tray with the cut surface upwards.

Repeat the pastry slathering, nut-spreading, rolling and cutting until you have produced enough small cylinders to fill your baking tray. Then bake in a 170 degrees C oven until the pastry is golden.

While the baklava is baking, prepare the syrup. Pour the honey into a saucepan with a few spoonfuls of water, and whatever other flavourings you fancy (see above for possibilities) and bring to the boil before taking off the heat.

When the baklava is out of the oven, pour the syrup over the nut pastries until the honey comes to the top of each cylinder. Leave to soak, and after a few hours most of the syrup will have been absorbed by the pastry and nuts. The longer you leave it, the better it will taste, up to about four days.

PEARS *EN PAPILLOTE*

I love this recipe because of the frisson of drama as the fruit is unwrapped, and also because it's just so easy.

For each person you're making it for you need:
greaseproof paper (something like 30cm x 30cm)
a piece of cotton string
one pear
some honey
some spirits such as raki*
whatever spices you're tempted by - cinnamon goes very well.

Peel each pear and cut the bottom so it sits in the middle of a square of baking parchment.

Drizzle honey over the outside of each pear and douse with a few tablespoons of raki or other spirits.

Sprinkle with cinnamon or other spices.

Bring the corners of the baking parchment together over each pear and tie a knot around the

parchment at the stalk. This should make a fancy looking (and watertight) parcel with a flared top.

Put in the oven and bake at 190 degrees C until the pear is soft - about half an hour.

Take out of the oven with a fanfare, and allow people to unwrap their own parcel on their plate.

Serve with ice-cream or crème fraîche.

*Raki is a spirit made in the Balkans usually from grapes or plums, but also very deliciously from quinces, for example. Grappa or calvados or anything similar would work.

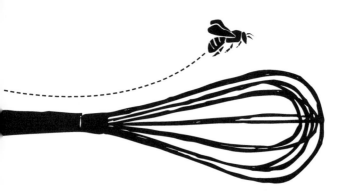

HONEY SPICE CAKE / *PAIN D'ÉPICES*

I loved every minute of making this cake - beginning
with the indulgence of a recipe which starts with
blending warm milk, honey and butter. Next you sift
the flour with the powder ingredients - first the smoky
trails as the flour tumbles through the sieve, then the
mixing of my favourite spices and the pounding of
cloves like a whisper of magic Christmas breath in my
cake.

As it baked, the house filled filled with a spectacular
scent but I can't pretend that the best bit wasn't once
it was out of the oven and cut into slices.

It's not as dark and sticky as the shop-bought *pain
d'épices* I've eaten but this is a great cake (or bread;
I tried a piece with butter and even, as a late-night
nibble, with cheese).

Ingredients:
¾ cup milk
¾ cup honey
3 cups plain flour
6 tbsp butter
2 tbsp sugar
2 tsp baking powder
1 tsp cinnamon
½ tsp ginger
¼ tsp allspice
¼ tsp ground cloves
1 egg, lightly beaten

Heat the milk in a small saucepan until warm to the touch. Add the honey and stir until blended. Stir in the butter until it is completely melted. Remove from the heat and cool until just warm.

In a large mixing bowl, sift the flour with the sugar, baking powder and spices.

Stir in the cooled milk mixture and egg; mix until well blended.

Butter and flour a 25cm loaf tin. Spread dough in the pan and bake at 170 degrees C for about an hour.

APPLE PIE WITH HONEY PASTRY

I'm an enthusiastic eater of pastry, but an incompetent pastry chef. My pastry cheffing is generally a botch job, squeezing together sudden unexpected fissures.

I don't know whether it's my science that's wrong, or my art. I know there is science to pastry-making (for my grandmother the final proof of the impossibility of the climate in Malaya was that she had to make her pastry there with her hands in the fridge). But my guess is that there's also something about panache and instinct and patience and careful application of muscle that I just don't have.

But I think – as with so many things – honey may have saved me. I read about honey pastry and I reckoned that it might be a more supple, more forgiving kind of pastry. And of course it would taste great so even if I ended up with my usual Frankenstein scene of torn patches I could bake them up and eat them separately.

Ingredients for the honey pastry:
5-6 tablespoons milk
1½ tablespoons honey
1 teaspoon salt
1 cup butter
2¾ cup flour

Mix milk and honey; dissolve salt in liquid. Cut butter into flour and blend into pea-sized clumps. Pour in the liquid and mix until dough is uniform. Divide dough in half, roll out and cut to fit tin. Prick bottom with a fork and bake at 230 degrees C for 8 minutes.

For the filling:
4 medium apples (chopped)
¾ cup honey
1 tbsp cinnamon
1 tsp vanilla
2 tablespoons butter to dot on top

Combine the filling ingredients and when the pastry case is baked, add the filling. Roll out (yes, just like that – really, it doesn't tear at all!) the remainder of the pastry for the lid. Crimp round the edges and make a vent in the top. Use any spare pastry for a creative decoration.

Bake at 230 degrees C for about 10 minutes or until golden brown (remembering that the honey in the pastry will make it brown sooner than normal pastry will).

HONEY ICE-CREAM

The urge for ice-cream comes on slow, sunny days, but making your own without an ice-cream maker is not usually a slow or sunny activity (all that constant returning to the freezer to bash at the ice crystals when you could be lolling in a garden, lulled by the buzz of bees). That's what's so brilliant about this recipe – it requires no machinery beyond an electric whisk, and no repeat trips to check on the freezer compartment. It comes courtesy of my parents' friend, Trish, who's lived in many countries where you can't rely on shop-bought ice-cream to come in anything other than salmonella flavour. This home-made alternative tastes delicious.

Ingredients:
4 eggs
⅓ cup sugar
2⅔ cups double cream
1 pot of honey – the runnier the better

Whip the eggs and the sugar together until they are white. (This doesn't mean whipping just the egg whites until they lose their transparency, but whipping the whole egg until it's white. This is where the electric whisk is essential. The air which is added to the eggs by doing this extensive whipping is the key factor in being able to have fluffy ice-cream without an ice-cream maker.)

Whip the cream until stiff, and fold in the honey.

Combine all the ingredients, folding carefully to keep in as much air as possible.

Freeze overnight. (I usually find this a rather strange recipe direction as it suggests that you would be eating the ice-cream first thing in the morning. But maybe homemade honey ice-cream could form the perfect indulgent breakfast.)

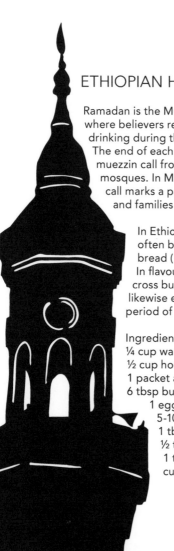

ETHIOPIAN HONEY BREAD

Ramadan is the Muslim month of fasting where believers refrain from eating or drinking during the hours of daylight. The end of each day's fast is signalled by muezzin call from the minarets of the mosques. In Muslim communities, that call marks a pause when businesses shut and families come together to eat.

In Ethiopia, the Ramadan fast is often broken with a spiced honey bread ('Yemarina yewotet dabo'). In flavour it reminds me of hot cross buns, which in England are likewise eaten at the end of the period of denial during Lent.

Ingredients:
¼ cup warm water
½ cup honey
1 packet active dried yeast
6 tbsp butter, melted
1 egg, beaten
5-10 cups flour
1 tbsp ground coriander
½ tsp ground cloves
1 tsp salt
cup lukewarm milk

Glaze:
1 egg
4 tbsp milk

In a small bowl, stir together water and honey (and maybe a pinch of sugar). Sprinkle in yeast and allow to sit in a warm place until frothy – about 10 minutes. Add butter and egg to yeast mixture.

In a separate bowl, sift most of the flour with coriander, cloves and salt. Stir in yeast mixture and milk, stirring and adding more flour until a firm dough forms.

Place dough on a floured surface and knead for about 20 minutes - until dough is smooth and stretches. Place dough in a lightly greased bowl, cover with a damp towel, and allow to rise until double in size, at least 90 minutes.

Knead the dough again and divide into 3 portions; roll each portion into a sausage shape and braid to form a loaf. Move the loaf to a well-greased baking sheet, cover with a damp towel and allow to rise in a warm place until double in size (approximately one hour).

To make glaze, combine egg with milk. Brush the top of the loaf with the glaze. Bake at 170 degrees C for about 30 minutes or until golden.

SHANDATLIE HONEY AND WALNUT CAKE

Like baklava (see p. 56) this dessert is structured around carbohydrate soaked in syrup. In baklava the carbohydrate in question is filo pastry but the principle is very similar as in shandatlie. As with baklava, you can try replacing some or all of the sugar for the syrup with honey for a more complex flavour.

Even with the walnuts to take the edge off the sweetness, this is cloying stuff. It goes well with some tart fruit such as raspberries or pomegranate seeds, and/ or with crème fraîche.

Ingredients:
3¾ cups of sugar
vanilla
4 eggs
6 tbsp butter
5 tbsp honey
¾ cup ground walnuts
3 cups flour
half tsp bicarbonate of soda

This recipe comes from the Hysa Albanian cookbook and makes approximately 8 servings.

Pre-heat the oven to 175 degrees C.

Mix together all the honey, walnuts, flour, bicarbonate of soda and 3 eggs, ¾ cup sugar and 4 tablespoons butter. Stir until just combined.

Pour the mixture into a greased baking tin. Brush the top with beaten egg and bake in the oven for 40 minutes.

While the cake is cooking, prepare the syrup. Stir 3 cups of sugar and the vanilla in 2¼ cups water, bring to the boil and cook until syrup spins a long thread.

Remove the cake from the oven, chill and cut into diamonds When the cake is chilled (and not before – I made this mistake, and ended up with a tin which sparkled with a solid crystalline crust), pour warm syrup over and allow 2 hours for the cake to soak up the syrup.

Serve cold.

SALEP – DRINKING ORCHIDS IN A TURKISH WINTER

For sheer oriental indulgence you can't beat the idea of a drink made with ground orchid root. This drink, sweetened with honey, is a typical sight on the streets of Istanbul in winter, where vendors sell it from large steaming copper urns.

For one mug of *salep*:
1 – 1½ tsp *salep* (the ground root, not the prepackaged drink to which you just add milk. The ground root is available in Turkish markets)
1 tsp honey
1 cup milk
½ tsp vanilla
cinnamon to serve

Boil the milk. Mix *salep* and honey in a bowl and blend it to a paste.

After the milk boils, lower the heat and gradually add the *salep* and honey mixture, stirring continually to prevent it becoming lumpy.

Boil on the lowest heat for half an hour and towards the end of this time, add vanilla. Pour into a cup and sprinkle cinnamon on it to taste.

HONEY VINAIGRETTE

Honey is not only successful in sweet recipes. This salad dressing recipe uses honey to undercut what would otherwise be too sour a vinaigrette, and this is one of those dressings I always hope will be left over so I can mop it up with bread at the end of the meal.

The best honeys for this are complex and not overly sweet – see, for example, the dandelion honey on page 28, or thistle honey (p. 35) or apple blossom honey (p. 40)

Mix together:
3 tsp lemon juice
1 tsp white wine vinegar
½ tsp honey
1 tbsp olive oil
pinch black pepper
pinch salt

FRENCH HONEYSUCKLE HONEY ICE LOLLIES

This is a strikingly pale honey which my honey dictionary tells me is ideal for making ice lollies. Rather uncertain about ice lolly technique, I tried putting into the freezer a teaspoon filled with the fudgy, lightly fragrant 'sulla' honey I'd been sent by the wonderful MieliThun company in Italy.

After leaving it for a few hours in the freezer I had a refreshing classy lollipop. Licked, it is a childish sweet treat; chewed, it's a more sophisticated creamy parfait with a light citrus floral taste. Summer on a spoon!

HONEY CRUMBLE – A DAIRY-FREE VERSION OF THE FRUIT PUDDING

Fruit crumble (or 'crisp' as it's called in America) is an easy, versatile dessert, like making a fruit pie (see p. 62) but stopping before you get to the tricky bit. But it's dependent on the rubbed-in butter to make the 'crumbs' of the topping, and as such isn't great for your cholesterol, your calories or your lactose-intolerant friends.

Honey offers a dairy-free alternative to holding together the crumb. Of course because of its sweetness it reduces the need for sugar too. This crumble works for all kinds of fruit, but is particularly great with apples, pears or plums.

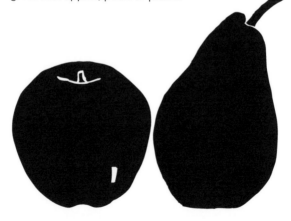

I like a deep crumble so this recipe has a higher crumble: fruit ratio than others you might come across. It makes approximately 4 servings.

Ingredients:
1 cooking apple, grated - or equivalent quantity of other fruit
1 cup oats or other breakfast cereal
⅔ cup plain flour
6 tbsp honey

Preheat oven to 150 degrees C. Place fruit in oven-proof dish with spice to taste (e.g. cinnamon/cloves/ginger).

Pour flour and oats into a bowl and rub honey into the mixture. Crumble this over the fruit. Bake for about 30 minutes, when fruit should be soft and topping browned.

FRIED DOUGH BALLS SOAKED IN HONEY SYRUP

This is one version of the Greek dish, *loukoumades*, where dough is balled, deep fried and soaked in honey syrup. The result is an extremely moreish brunch dish.

Ingredients:
1¾ cups plain flour
3 tbsp warm water
3 tbsp milk
1½ tbsp melted butter
2 tsp baking powder
oil for deep frying
½ cup honey*
juice and zest of ½ lemon
cinnamon to sprinkle

*Greek pine honey is ideal (see p. 38)

To form the syrup, mix together the honey and lemon in a flat dish.

Then combine the flour, water, milk, melted butter and baking powder until it makes a stiff dough (you may have to add more flour to get the right consistency).

Form small balls the size of cherries and deep-fry in the oil until they are golden brown. The balls will swell up to about 3 times their size, which is fun to watch.

Drain the balls and set in the syrup, sprinkling with cinnamon to taste. This recipe makes about 22 dough balls.

HONEYED POPCORN

More than gold, more than guns, the item with the highest mark-up on the market is… popcorn. You take a few spoonfuls of one of the world's most basic foodstuffs – maize kernels – and combine with some oil and heat, and then sell in a Cineworld foyer for £6.35 for 100 grams! Nice one.

Or you can make your own. It's cheap, and you can't deny it's fun – the miniature explosions of small grains turning their insides out, and creating tiny puffs of brain-shaped sponge in the process; the moment you discover that the lid wasn't on properly, and all the tiny puffs of brain-shaped sponge are in your hair…

You can then flavour your popcorn with whatever you like. One favourite of mine is serving it up with a toothpick and a small ramekin of Nutella.

You can sneer if you like, but you know you want to try it. Or melting a little peanut butter and tossing the popcorn in that? Delicious. But best (and maybe most healthy) of all has got to be honeying the popcorn.

Ingredients:
1 tbsp sunflower oil
30g popping corn
4 tbsp honey
60g butter

Heat the oil in a large pan, stir in the corn, cover and shake the pan constantly over heat until the popping stops. Remove the corn from the pan and cool. Place the corn in a lightly-greased baking tin.

Combine the honey and butter in a saucepan. Stir over low heat until the butter is melted. Bring to the boil, then boil on medium heat for approximately 5 minutes.

Pour the honey mixture over the corn, and stir to coat well. Leave to set as long as you can bear.

TIESSENNAU MEL
WELSH HONEY MUFFINS

These delicious Welsh honey cakes are made in muffin tins but they're as dark as parkin, as sticky as gingerbread. This recipe makes 12 muffins.

Ingredients:
½ cup butter
½ cup brown sugar
1 egg
½ cup honey
1 cup flour
1 tsp cinnamon
½ tsp bicarbonate of soda
¼ cup milk
icing sugar

Grease muffin tins (not forgetting to grease around the top where the 'muffin tops' will easily stick).

Melt the butter and mix with the sugar, honey and egg.

Combine flour with cinnamon and bicarb of soda; add to butter mixture, alternating with milk.

Fill muffin tins less than halfway and sprinkle icing sugar on top. Bake at 200 degrees C for 20 minutes or until a toothpick comes out clean.

MISCELL-
HONEY

THE HONEY PLEDGE; SUBSTITUTING FOR SUGAR

The carbon footprint of local honey is practically zero. Indeed, given the role of the honey-producers in pollinating plants, I reckon my jar of honey takes you into carbon credit. I harvest my honey with a creaking hand-powered centrifuge and I package it in recycled jam jars; I feel virtuous with every sweet spoonful I feed myself.

And of course it tastes great, and better than alternative forms of sweetener. Sugar is to honey what white noise is to music; the uncomplicated sheer sweetness of the white stuff is reliable but ultimately gives me a headache, while honey adds subtlety. It's better for you, too – research (Phillips, Carlsen and Blomhoff, 2009)

reckoned that substituting honey for sugar increases antioxidants in the diet by the equivalent of an extra serving of berries or nuts every day. Bite me.

So I took a pledge a few years ago that I wouldn't use sugar any more. I stir honey into herbal tea, and I drizzle honey over cereal, and I have learned to use honey in baking.

That takes a bit of practice, and a few tricks, but it's worth it. Honey has a slight acidity which has to be offset in baking with a little extra bicarb of soda. Honey is also obviously a little more liquid which means you have to adjust the amounts of liquid you use elsewhere in a recipe. And it leads to cakes browning more quickly so you have to aim off for that with the oven temperature. But these are all small adjustments, and you work them out with a bit of instinct and a bit of trial and error – more art than science.

Are you ready to take the honey pledge?

HONEY FACE CREAM AND THE REFUGE FOR TRAFFICKED WOMEN WHERE IT'S MADE

This isn't something you eat – although it looks and smells almost good enough to do so. This is honey mixed with propolis (the antiseptic gathered by bees from the shiny coating of buds and used as all-purpose fixer and filler in the hive) and some other magic and prepared as a face cream to be worn overnight.

So in the early hours of the morning I will slather this form of honey on my face, not on a piece of toast.

It's pretty special honey (hopefully will make me look pretty/ special), harvested in hives managed by

women from the Safe House (Shtëpia e sigurt) in the western Kosovo town of Gjakova. The Safe House offers refuge for women who are the victims of human trafficking or survivors of domestic violence, and while they are staying there they are given training and tools to rebuild their lives. They're offered counselling and English classes and IT tutorials and… beekeeping. I love the idea of this community of women where each manages a community of women, casting themselves as queen bee; I can see the poetry that's more than just punning when a girl dons a veil and really feels inviolable when she's wearing it. It's a powerful metaphor, as well as being a powerful opportunity for financial independence if a woman can run a small business like beekeeping.

In the short term while the women are in training in the Shtëpia e sigurt, the honey (and the face creams it's made with) are sold to raise money for the Safe House itself. I've bought pots of the stuff.

THE FORAGER'S TREAT

When beekeepers tell you just how complex is the art and science of looking after a hive, it is amazing to discover just how well the bees can get on on their own. There are still plenty of wild swarms in the UK, and although raiding for a lick of honey may not be your first thought if you come by surprise across a bee hive, it's the idea of such sweet abundance freely available which makes bee hives seem such luxurious examples of nature's bounty. Honey is the ultimate foraging treat.

Whether your honey is bought from a shop (or a local beekeeper) or raided in the wild, a foraging spree to see what else Mother Nature provides for free will give you not only a sense of self-sufficiency but also the perfect wild accompaniment to eat with the honey.

Find sage or chamomile and boil the leaves/
flowers respectively to make wholesome
teas whose slight bitterness is well offset by
honey.

Or pick elderflowers and boil them up with
lemon and honey to make a cordial which can
then be diluted for a refreshing summer drink.

Later in the year, of course, it's blackberry season,
and the blackberries can be preserved by soaking in
a light liquid honey which makes a great spread for
bread or toast.

None of this will cost you anything, and the food miles
involved, and the carbon cost, will be zero.

Bon appétit!

TREATED LIKE ROYALTY

Royal jelly is a nutritious substance produced for the nourishment of the queen bee in each hive. The fact that queen bees live 40 times longer than the worker bees who are not fed with the royal jelly rich in protein, vitamins and minerals, has led to it being credited with rejuvenating and health-giving powers (I took it myself when I had glandular fever, and quickly recovered – though of course no control group was available).

In Kosovo I visited a royal jelly commercial producer. Bajram Bajrami is deeply serious about royal jelly and when he asks me whether I'd like to try some combined in a special healthy bee-product cocktail he has devised, it is submitting to an earnest and just slightly spooky ritual. After all, I am to be fed with the excretions destined for an insect monarch; and standing in the cool dim basement where Bajram keeps his honey, there is a touch of the cloister, or the catacomb.

'You must take it from a wooden spoon,' advises

Bajram, though I don't understand the reason he gives for this. He passes me a wooden spoon with a slick of a dull brown sludge on it. Obediently I put it in my mouth.

Strangely, given the discussion about our cutlery, my first sensation is of a metallic taste. It's slightly granular and creamier than honey and it's not unpleasant, but nor is it easy to swallow. It definitely feels like it's doing you some good.

'Er, and what's in it?' I ask.

Bajram tells me this is crystallized mountain honey mixed with pollen and royal jelly. I should take a spoonful every morning, he tells me, and I will be perfectly healthy. I wonder whether, as the day goes on, I will feel delusions of grandeur, or start to boss others around. Nourishing my inner queen could be a risky business.

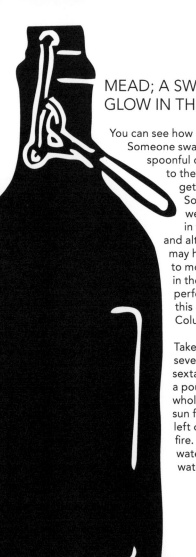

MEAD; A SWEET ANCIENT GLOW IN THE MOUTH

You can see how mead was developed. Someone swallowed a delicious spoonful of honey and thought to themselves 'I'd like to get drunk on this stuff'. So sticky experiments were conducted there in the ancient kitchen, and although a few people may have been sacrificed to moonshine blindness, in the end the recipe was perfected. Something like this one from the Roman, Columella:

Take rainwater kept for several years, and mix a sextarius of this water with a pound of honey. … The whole is exposed to the sun for 40 days, and then left on a shelf near the fire. If you have no rain water, then boil spring water.

From *Beowulf* I associate mead more with Anglo-Saxon than with Classical drunkenness. But mead is still commercially available today, and small producers have some interesting ways of combining honey and alcohol, including delicious fruit meads (technically, the additional of fruit means these are not meads but melomels. I like just saying that word; I can imagine myself after a certain number of glasses of 14.5% ABV melomel simply sitting with a soft stupid smile repeating melomelomelomelomel…).

In fact, many of the names for honey and alcohol combinations have something magical in the sound. One I've never tried is acerglyn – a mead made from honey and maple syrup. It's probably a delicious drink, but it could also be the name of a wizard. Bochet is a version where the honey is caramelized before being added to the water. Braggot is a Welsh version with malt added (I imagine Bochet and Braggot would be the arch-enemies of Wizard Acerglyn). Metheglin is a mead with herbs and spices added – and in my honey fantasy world this would be the name for the woman with whom Acerglyn is infatuated.

What the drinks have in common is an aftertaste that's soft, warming and distinctly honeyed. You're left with no sharpness, just a sweet glow inside your mouth. Perhaps it is a folk memory of companionable drinking going back through Tolkien, through ancient Rome and Greece and to something very very old in the appetites of the human race.

BZZZZ BRRRR.
A BEE FONDANT
RECIPE

Over the winter bees keep
alive by forming a ball in
the centre of the hive. The
temperature of a beehive
is the same as the human
body and the bees work
as a team to maintain this
temperature. They take it in
turns to be on the outside
of the ball where it is colder,
and when they are getting
very cold they circulate into
the centre of the ball where
the accumulated body heat
of thousands of bees warms
them until it is time again
for them to take their turn at
the extremity, exposed to the
winter. I imagine this being
rather like a huge tremulous

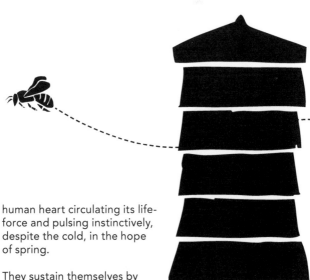

human heart circulating its life-
force and pulsing instinctively,
despite the cold, in the hope
of spring.

They sustain themselves by
eating the honey that they
worked so hard to store up
over the summer. Of course, the wicked humans have
removed some of this honey for their own sticky ends,
but if the beekeeper has done a good job she has left
enough honey to see the bees through winter. If she
has calculated wrong then some energy supplies need
to be added to the hive. This can be sugar syrup or a
paste called 'bee fondant', the recipe for which is one
part liquid honey to two parts icing sugar. You can lay
this on the hive in a large sustaining slab, rather like
icing an exotic cake. And yes, if you're feeling in need
of a few extra calories yourself, you can nibble a bit,
just to keep your strength up.

DRIZZLERS

Honey from a drizzler: it's the languorous teatime way to eat. Watching the faery columns of gold spooling down from a drizzler is like being allowed to play with your food. Or like meditating – and knowing you'll be immediately rewarded with a sweet treat.

But how did this particular design come about for transferring honey? When I've told beekeepers in other countries that we have a special implement for moving honey from jar to plate they look incredulous, much as I would look if I were told there was a particular tool for peanut butter, or a carefully curved 'Marmite knife'. I wonder whether there might be something of the stout body and stripes of apis mellifera in the way the wood is turned; or maybe something borrowed from the skep – the egg-shaped woven hives that bees were kept in traditionally?

Whatever the origins, this is the way to add drama to your honey-eating.

ABOUT
THIS
BOOK

ELIZABETH

After many years of practising honey-eating, I finally became a honey-harvester/ hobby beekeeper five years ago. I was living in Kosovo at the time and the story of my experiences is told in my book, *Travels in Blood and Honey; becoming a beekeeper in Kosovo* (designed by Su and Paddy and published by Signal Books in 2011). The book includes recipes I learned to make with my honey, and the process of writing it opened my eyes and my tastebuds to honey's possibilities. This *Little Book of Honey* shares some of the adventures I've had since then.

When I'm not eating honey, I work as one of the three founders of the Kosovan charity, The Ideas Partnership (www.theideaspartnership.org), running educational, environmental and cultural heritage projects. I'm also busy (as a ...) finishing my next book, *Edith and I; adventures with an Edwardian traveller in Kosovo,* telling the story of following the trail of an extraordinary writer, anthropologist and aid worker in the Balkans a century ago.

www.elizabethgowing.com

SU AND PADDY

Originally from Shropshire/Dublin we are graphic designers who now live and work in Yorkshire (land of heather honey).

Paddy teaches on the graphics course at the University of Leeds and Su is a product developer for a major high street retailer. Our favourite things are food, walking and photography and travel adventures that combine these three passions.

We first met Elizabeth when we were all volunteers on a summer project in Albania. Since then the three of us have collaborated on *Travels in Blood and Honey; becoming a beekeeper in Kosovo* (Signal Books, 2011, which Elizabeth wrote and we designed) and on other volunteering projects in the Balkans, including This is Neighbourhood 29 (www.neighbourhood29. com) where Roma children in Kosovo were supported to present their community through beautifully vivid photographs, later presented in a high-profile exhibition.

www.mcentaggart.co.uk

Praise for *Travels in Blood and Honey; becoming a beekeeper in Kosovo*

Elizabeth, Su and Paddy's previous collaboration was published by Signal Books in 2011.

'A sheer delight' - *The Times*

'As fresh, rich and fluid as the honey Ms Gowing harvests' – *The Lady*

'Compulsively readable' - *The Beekeepers' Quarterly*

'Enthralling... a wonderful evocation of a place that most of us know so little about. Food, above all honey, is the key that unlocks the doors between cultures.' – Sophie Grigson

'A fantastic read! ... wonderful stories and experiences, with delicious recipes inter-woven.' Celebrity chef Lesley Waters

Gourmand World Cookbook Awards UK Winner

For stockists of some of the honeys mentioned here, and to take you on your own honey adventures, try:

www.honeypacifica.com
particularly for the rare avocado honey (see p. 12)

www.karasardegna.it
for asphodel honey (see p. 36)

www.mielithun.it
the website of an organisation inspiringly passionate about an astonishing range of quality honey

www.nzartisanhoney.co.nz
for viper's bugloss honey (p. 23) and more

Planet Organic shops
for Regent's Park honey (p. 20)

Other interesting honey links for more information on projects mentioned in the text:

www.beesabroad.org.uk
for relief of poverty through beekeeping in developing countries (see p. 30)

www.thegoldenco-op.com
for the Golden Company's Hackney project (see p. 34)

And for a wealth of more honey recipes, collected by the Professor of Entomology at the University of Illinois, see *Honey I'm Homemade: sweet treats from the beehive across the centuries and around the world* by May Berenbaum.

CONVERSIONS

1 cup flour = 150g
1 cup sugar = 225g
1 cup butter = 225g
1 cup honey = 350g
1tbsp = 15ml